Peace Prayers

All royalties from the sale of this book will be donated to:

Children's Defense Fund

Doctors Without Borders

UNICEF

Peace Prayers

Meditations, Affirmations, Invocations, Poems, and Prayers for Peace

Edited by the staff of Harper San Francisco
Carrie Leadingham, Joann E. Moschella, and Hilary M. Vartanian

HarperSanFrancisco
A Division of HarperCollins*Publishers*

 For information address HarperCollins Publishers, 10 East 53rd Street, New York, NY 10022.

FIRST EDITION

Library of Congress Cataloging-in-Publication Data

Peace prayers : meditations, affirmations, invocations, poems, and prayers for peace. —1st ed.
p. cm.
Includes index.
ISBN 0-06-250464-9 (alk. paper)
1. Peace—Religious aspects—Meditations. 2. Prayers for peace.
3. War-Quotations, maxims, etc.
BL65.P4P33 1992
291.1'7873—dc20 91-55295
CIP

---

92 93 94 95 96 ❖ K.P. 10 9 8 7 6 5 4 3 2 1

This edition is printed on acid-free paper that meets the American National Standards Institute Z39.48 Standard.

Harper San Francisco, in association
with the Rainforest Action Network, will facilitate
the planting of two trees for every one tree used
in the manufacture of this book.

Contents

Publisher's Foreword

Most books grow out of the passions of our authors. This book, conceived in the midst of the conflicting emotions swirling around the early stages of the 1991 Gulf War, grew from a passion that arose within a publishing house. A passion for the power inherent in words.

At the moment of this book's conception, the rhetoric of war was a deafening clamor. All words of peace seemed to be regarded as evidence of sentimentality, weakness, or, at worst, a lack of patriotism. For many of us, particularly those for whom a country unified in favor of war was a new experience, it was an unsettling time. The rhetoric of war so overwhelmed the gentle words of peace, that one could easily lose faith in the power and potential of peace itself.

As we solicited material, this book grew to reflect the questions that inevitably surround conflicts and the elusive concept of peace. We discovered that the problem of peace cannot be encapsulated easily in the sincere but naive language of a slogan. On the contrary, those who pursue peace have chosen to follow the most demanding and courageous of paths. True peace seekers discover that what often serves to drive the world apart—religion, race, gender—can give them the strength to fight the easier impulse to make war.

As disparate images and ideas found their way together, it became ironically clear that a book that effectively addresses peace must first present the image of a world at war. "With Whom Shall We Live?" opens the book with this loss of peace. What happens to a soldier when his "enemy" on the other side of the battle becomes human? What are the consequences when that soldier says, "no more"? Through trying to understand the ramifications of war and the difficulties of peace, we begin to see that the enemy is within us, the insidious enemy that is fear of the unknown or the other.

"Silence Abides" makes clear that the hope for global peace begins with each individual's deep thirst for interior peace. Without an understanding of the conflicting natures within our own souls, we can do little to quell the violence outside of us. We realize along with Simone Weil that "we contain the seeds of every crime."

Peace is more than the space between wars. "Mindfulness Must Be Engaged" presents us with the uncomfortable truth that peace is not merely the lack of conflict. For all those who use the abstract idea of peace to escape from the harsh reality of injustice, there are active peacemakers who use it to rattle the bars of enslaving complacency.

We are still left with the question, "what exactly is peace?" "Shelter Beneath the Tree" is a common anthem that sings out the desire for what we have come to call peace. Although often intangible, there is a demand for peace that springs from the collective soul of all nations. It is a universal desire that exists because, as Tolstoy claimed, "it is written in our minds and hearts."

We hope that these prayers and thoughts are not just inspiring but enabling. Let us go about the business of peace.

Clayton E. Carlson
Memorial Day
1991

Defenceless under the night
Our world in stupor lies;
Yet, dotted everywhere,
Ironic points of light
Flash out wherever the Just
Exchange their messages:
May I, composed like them
Of Eros and of dust,
Beleaguered by the same
Negation and despair,
Show an affirming flame.

—W. H. Auden

With Whom Shall We Live?

There is many a boy here today who looks on war as all glory but, boys, it is all hell.

WILLIAM T. SHERMAN

The Corpse

The corpse was there, brothers and sisters,
and no one's eyes wept.
We felt no pain nor did we pretend,
we didn't notice its rags
nor the rigid stillness of its jaws.
We proceeded without seeing it, we disowned it,
we didn't know its name, we didn't inquire,
we simply continued without looking.
We were terrorized with so much death,
that blood of our blood now caused no grief.
It remained alone, thrown in the middle of the street,
its open eyes an accusation.

MARIA ISABEL DE LOS ANGELES RUANO

I have seen war. I have seen war on land and sea. I have seen blood running from the wounded. I have seen men coughing out their gassed lungs. I have seen the dead in the mud. I have seen cities destroyed.

I have seen 200 limping, exhausted men come out of the line—the survivors of a regiment of a thousand that went forward 48 hours before. I have seen children starving. I have seen the agony of mothers and wives. I hate war.

FRANKLIN D. ROOSEVELT

A Diary Without Dates

I, no sense of being alive,
live next door to death.

My neck was so feeble,
it toppled if anyone touched it.
I felt I had turned to stone.

Every day my anxiety grew deeper,
until it enveloped me so thickly
that I could see nothing.
Alone in an illimitable desert

I wept hopelessly, as if in a nightmare in
    dawn
where the open mouthed blue sky wept
    with me.

The trees wept,
a bird's body,
a horse's bleached bones,
all spell bound.
Immobile, watched with bated breath
the figure of death.

The world was unbearably still.
I sat side by side with death,
held immobile in reality,
only hoping I would not fall.

NAKAMURA CHIO

The "peace" that prevails today is the peace of fear and the peace of preparation. Ignoring the sincere advice of men of wisdom, the great nations of the world are intent upon demonstration of their destructive strength. That way lies war, not peace.

SWAMI SIVANANDA

Society was divided into warring camps suspicious of one another. Where no contract or obligation was binding, nothing could heal the conflict, and since security was only to be found in the assumption that nothing was secure, everyone took steps to preserve himself and no one could afford to trust his neighbor.

THUCYDIDES

Weapon

The will to power destroys the power to will.
The weapon made, we cannot help but use it;
it drags us with its own momentum still.

The power to kill compounds the need to kill.
Grown out of hand the heart cannot refuse it;
the will to power undoes the power to will.

Though as we strike we cry, "I did not choose it,"
it drags us with its own momentum still.
In the one stroke we win the world and lose it.
The will to power destroys the power to will.

JUDITH WRIGHT

Perhaps we are at last coming to see that our most deadly enemy is fear. We are frightened almost to death by our ingenious hostility, which has wired the earth for genocide. We cannot conquer that enemy; we can only be delivered from it by love in the form of trust. Gandhi knew that the only safe way to overcome an enemy is to make of the enemy a friend. Are we capable of receiving the gift on which our cure depends?

JIM WALLIS

The Prayer of Jonah (or: the futility of hatred)

Out of my distress I called you, O Lord,
but you did not answer me.

I refused to preach repentance to the Ninevites,
but you forced me.

When I sailed away in the opposite direction,
you hurled a violent wind at me.
Your monster swallowed me and returned me to your path.

Repentance I would not preach in Nineveh,
rather I cursed them, "Forty days more and Nineveh shall be destroyed."

But you did not listen to me.
You listened to the people of Nineveh as they sat in ashes
covered with sackcloth.

I am angry because you are a gracious and merciful God,
slow to anger,
rich in clemency,
loathe to punish.

If you will not destroy Nineveh then give me death.
It is better for me to die than to see my enemy live.

THOMAS REESE, S.J.

Tribal

Our tribal god
With mouth of fire
Still slays our foes
At our desire.
Our bloody axe
He loves to bless,
And give our cause
His righteousness.

In painted caves
They stand arrayed.
The gods of stone
That hurt or aid.
Our flag is his.
And when we kill
We but obey
His holy will.
Our churches hang
Blood trophies up
Where Piety lifts
The Sacred Cup.
In painted caves
They stand arrayed.
The gods of stone
That hurt or aid.
"Thou shalt not kill,"
We write in blood,
And whet the spear
Before the Rood.
In painted caves
They stand arrayed.
The gods of stone
That hurt or aid.

Oh, magic stones
The tribes are met,
And shrapnel screams
O'er Olivet.

MARY FULLERTON

The War Prayer

Listen!
"O Lord our Father,
our young patriots, idols of our hearts,
go forth to battle—
be Thou near them!
With them, in spirit,
we also go forth from the sweet peace of our beloved firesides
to smite the foe.

O Lord our God,
help us to tear their soldiers to bloody shreds with our shells;
help us to cover their smiling fields
with the pale forms of their patriot dead;
help us to drown the thunder of the guns
with the shrieks of their wounded, writhing in pain;
Help us to lay waste their humble homes

with a hurricane of fire;
help us to wring the hearts of their unoffending widows
with unavailing grief;
help us to turn them out roofless
with their little children
to wander unfriended the wastes of their desolated land
in rags and hunger and thirst,
sports of the sun flames of summer and the icy winds of winter,
broken in spirit, worn with travail,
imploring Thee for the refuge of the grave
and denied it—
For our sakes who adore Thee, Lord,
blast their hopes,
blight their lives,
protract their bitter pilgrimage,
make heavy their steps,
water their way with their tears,
stain the white snow with the blood of their wounded feet!

We ask it,
in the spirit of love,
of Him Who is the Source of Love,
and Who is the ever-faithful refuge and friend
of all that are sore beset

and seek His aid
with humble and contrite hearts.
Amen.

Mark Twain

[War is] a crime. Ask the infantry and ask the dead.

Ernest Hemingway

Our Father, says he;
O hardened wretch! can you call him Father, when you are just going to cut your brother's throat?

Hallowed be they name:
how can the name of God be more impiously unhallowed, than by mutual bloody murder among you, his sons?

Thy kingdom come:
do you pray for the coming of his kingdom,
while you are endeavoring to establish an earthly despotism,
by spilling the blood of God's sons and subjects?

Thy will be done on earth as it is in heaven:
his will in heaven is for peace, but you are now meditating war.

Dare you to say to your Father in heaven:
Give us this day our daily bread,
when you are going, the next minute perhaps, to burn up your brother's corn-fields,
and had rather lose the benefit of them yourself,
than suffer him to enjoy them unmolested?

With what face can you say,
Forgive us our trespasses
as we forgive them that trespass against us,
when, so far from forgiving your own brother,
you are going,
with all the haste you can,
to murder him in cold blood,
for an alleged trespass that, after all, is but imaginary?

Do you presume to deprecate the danger of temptation, who,
not without great danger to yourself,
are doing all you can to force your brother into danger?
Do you deserve to be delivered from evil,
that is, from the evil being,
to whose impulse you submit yourself,
and by whose spirit you are now guided,
in contriving the greatest possible evil to your brother?

ERASMUS

Dear God,
with you everything is possible.
Let the cup of war,
killing, and destruction,
the cup of bloodshed,
human anguish and desolation,
the cup of torture,
breakage in human relationships and abandonment . . .
Dear God,
let this cup pass us by.
We are afraid.
We are trembling in the depths of our being.
We feel the sweat and tears
of thousands of people all over the world,
people who are afraid—
afraid to fight,
afraid to kill,
afraid of being killed,
afraid of an uncertain future.

Henri J. M. Nouwen

One

Speak your truth.
Listen when others speak theirs, too.
When you let go of fear, you will learn to love others,
and you will let them love you.
Do not be afraid of dying.
But do not be afraid to live.
Ask yourself what that means.
Open your heart to love, for that is why you're here.
And know that you are, and always have been One
with Me and all who live.

MELODY BEATTIE

Mother in Wartime

As if it were some noble thing,
She spoke of sons at war,
As if freedom's cause
Were pled anew at some heroic bar,
As if the weapons used today
Killed with great élan,
As if technicolor banners flew
To honor modern man—

Believing everything she read
In the daily news,
(No in-between to choose)
She thought that only
One side won,
Not that *both*
Might lose.

LANGSTON HUGHES

Behind every war there is a big lie. . . . The big lie behind all murder, from the random street killing to the efficient ovens of Auschwitz, to the even more efficient hydrogen bomb, is that the victims deserve to die.

JIM WALLIS

Dulce et decorum est

Bent double, like old beggars under sacks,
Knock-kneed, coughing like hags, we cursed through sludge,
Till on the haunting flares we turned our backs
And towards our distant rest began to trudge.
Men marched asleep. Many had lost their boots
But limped on, blood-shod. All went lame; all blind;

Drunk with fatigue; deaf even to the hoots
Of tired, outstripped Five-Nines that dropped behind.

Gas! Gas! Quick, boys!—An ecstasy of fumbling,
Fitting the clumsy helmets just in time;
But someone still was yelling out and stumbling,
And floundring like a man in fire or lime . . .
Dim, through the misty panes and thick green light,
As under a green sea, I saw him drowning.

In all my dreams, before my helpless sight,
He plunges at me, guttering, choking, drowning.

If in some smothering dreams you too could pace
Behind the wagon that we flung him in,
And watch the white eyes writhing in his face,
His hanging face, like a devil's sick of sin;
If you could hear, at every jolt, the blood
Come gargling from the froth-corrupted lungs,
Obscene as cancer, bitter as the cud
Of vile, incurable sores on innocent tongues,—
To children ardent for some desperate glory,
The old Lie: Dulce et decorum est
Pro patria mori.*

WILFRED OWEN

*It is sweet and beautiful to die for one's country.

The Warrior Caste has the ability to reproduce itself from one generation to the next. Only women can produce children, of course; but—more to the point—only wars can produce warriors. One war leads to the next, in part because each war incubates the warriors who will fight the next, or, I should say, create, the next. Our task—we who cherish "daily life" and life itself—is to end the millennia-old reign of the Warrior Caste. There are two parts to this task. One is to uproot the woman-hating, patriarchal consciousness that leads some men to find transcendence and even joy in war, and only war. That will take time, though we have made a decent start. The other part is to remember that war itself is the crucible in which new warriors are created. If we cannot stop the warriors' fevered obsessions, and bring these men back into the human fold, we can at least try to stop their wars.

BARBARA EHRENREICH

Call for Truthful Communication Leading to Peace

Oh Great Spirit,
this is a Call for Peace across the land,
so it is directed to the only Earth Dwellers
who are capable of making war
and have done so since their beginning.

I thank you, oh Creator
for allowing the powerful discoveries
that allow two-leggeds to reach
into all nooks and crannies,
glades, caverns, depths and valleys.

We thank you for the Age of Communication
which many of us understand to be the power
that will lead to a lasting peace.

No longer can the forked tongued ones,
those greedy and power questing two-legged;
no longer can they hide
all things that reflect the path of Truth.
You have allowed talking wires,
the voices that sing through the wind,
and even pictures of truth that go out into the depth of space
and bounce back beyond the rim of the Earth Mother,
in order that we will not be deceived.
In many lands now,
we two-legged are allowed to inscribe our winter counts (books)
truthfully as it was when we red two-legged inscribed them upon
the hides of our four-legged cousins.

When we see the Red Dawn rising in the East;
you are telling us that each new day will bring new knowledge.

I thank you for allowing your powers to help us tell what is truthfully happening.
We understand that knowledge unaltered and not distorted, can become wisdom
and that wisdom can lead to understanding.
Through such truthful observation and consideration,
we will win out some day and find an everlasting peace.

EAGLE MAN

In peace the sons bury their fathers
and in war the fathers bury their sons.

FRANCIS BACON

Come Up from the Fields Father

Come up from the fields father, here's a letter from
 our Pete,
And come to the front door mother, here's a letter from
 thy dear son.

Lo, 'tis autumn,
Lo, where the trees, deeper green, yellower and redder,
Cool and sweeten Ohio's villages with leaves fluttering in the
 moderate wind,
Where apples ripe in the orchards hang and grapes on
 the trellis'd vines,
(Smell you the smell of the grapes on the vines?
Smell you the buckwheat where the bees were lately
 buzzing?)

Above all, lo, the sky so calm, so transparent after the
 rain, and with wondrous clouds,
Below too, all calm, all vital and beautiful, and the farm
 prospers well.

Down in the fields all prospers well,
But now from the fields come father, come at the
 daughter's call,

And come to the entry mother, to the front door come
right away.

Fast as she can she hurries, something ominous, her steps
trembling,
She does not tarry to smooth her hair nor adjust her cap.

Open the envelope quickly,
O this is not our son's writing, yet his name is sign'd,
O a strange hand writes for our dear son, O stricken
mother's soul!
All swims before her eyes, flashes with black, she catches
the main words only,
Sentences broken, *gunshot wound in the breast, cavalry
skirmish, taken to hospital,*
At present low, but will soon be better.

Ah now the single figure to me,
Amid all teeming and wealthy Ohio with all its cities and
farms,
Sickly white in the face and dull in the head, very faint,
By the jamb of a door leans.

Grieve not so, dear mother, (the just-grown daughter
speaks through her sobs,

The little sisters huddle around speechless and dismay'd,)
See, dearest mother, the letter says Pete will soon be better.

Alas poor boy, he will never be better, (nor may-be needs to be better, that brave and simple soul,)
While they stand at home at the door he is dead already,
The only son is dead.

But the mother needs to be better,
She with thin form presently drest in black,
By day her meals untouch'd then at night fitfully sleeping, often waking,
In the midnight waking, weeping, longing with one deep longing,
O that she might withdraw unnoticed, silent from life escape and withdraw,
To follow, to seek, to be with her dear dead son.

WALT WHITMAN

Every gun that is made,
every warship launched,
every rocket fired signifies,
in the final sense,
a theft from those who hunger and are not fed,
those who are cold and are not clothed.

This world in arms is not spending money alone.
It is spending the sweat of its laborers,
the genius of its scientists,
the hopes of its children.

DWIGHT D. EISENHOWER

In olden times when there was a war, it was a human-to-human confrontation. The victor in battle would directly see the blood and suffering of the defeated enemy.

Nowadays, it is much more terrifying because a man in an office can push a button and kill millions of people and never see the human tragedy he has created.

The mechanization of war, the mechanization of human conflict, poses an increasing threat to peace.

THE DALAI LAMA

War is only a cowardly escape from the problems of peace.

THOMAS MANN

If you succumb to the temptation of using violence in the struggle, unborn generations will be the recipients of a long and desolate night of bitterness, and your chief legacy to the future will be an endless reign of meaningless chaos.

MARTIN LUTHER KING, JR.

Right from the moment of our birth, we are under the care and kindness of our parents. And then later on in our life, when we are oppressed by sickness and become old, we are again dependent on the kindness of others. And since at the beginning and end of our lives, we are so dependent on others' kindness, how can it be in the middle that we neglect kindness towards others?

THE DALAI LAMA

We say: killing is disorder, life and gentleness and community and unselfishness is the only order we recognize. The time is past when good men can remain silent, when obedience can segregate men from public risk, when the poor can die without defense.

How many must die before our voices are heard? How many must be tortured, dislocated, starved, maddened? How long must the world's resources be raped in the service of legalized murder? When, at what point, will you say no to this war?

DANIEL BERRIGAN, S.J.

War

The face of war is my face.
The face of war is your face.
What color
Is the face
Of war?
Brown, black, white—
Your face and my face.

Death is the broom
I take in my hands
To sweep the world
Clean.

I sweep and I sweep
Then mop and I mop.
I dip my broom in blood,
My mop in blood—
And blame you for this,
Because you are *there,*
Enemy.

It's hard to blame me,
Because I am here—
So I kill you.
And you kill me.
    My name,
Like your name,
    Is war.

LANGSTON HUGHES

The Sacred Pipe

With this pipe you will be bound to all your relatives:
your Grandfather and Father,
your Grandmother and Mother.
This round rock,

which is made of the same red stone as the bowl of the pipe,
your Father Wakan-Tanka has also given to you.
It is the Earth, your Grandmother and Mother,
and it is where you will live and increase.
This Earth which He has given to you is red,
and the two-leggeds who live upon the Earth are red;
and the Great Spirit has also given to you a red day,
and a red road.
All of this is sacred and so do not forget!
Every dawn as it comes is a holy event,
and every day is holy,
for the light comes from your Father Wakan-Tanka;
and also you must always remember that the two-leggeds and all the other peoples who stand upon this earth are sacred and should be treated as such.

OGLALA SIOUX RITUAL

We are one, after all, you and I;
together we suffer,
together exist,
and forever will recreate each other.

PIERRE TEILHARD DE CHARDIN

Magistrate:	You haven't any idea of what a war means.
Lysistrata:	We know just twice as well.
	We bore the sons
	You took for soldiers.
Magistrate:	Must you recall
	Such painful memories?
Lysistrata:	Yes.

ARISTOPHANES

Lament

Before time began I was there waiting to give birth.
I am the mother.
I gave birth to Osiris the bright one in the morning of the world.
I saw him die by the hand of his brother and I understood for,
I am the mother.
I suckled Orpheus the musician beside the wine dark sea,
I gathered up his body rent by frenzied hands and wept for,
I am the mother.
I bore Isaac in the time of my old age in the tents of Abraham
I stood silent when he was bound
and laid upon the sacred altar for,
I am the mother.
I laboured of a man child, whilst remaining a maid in Bethlehem

I uttered not a cry when they nailed him to a cross,
stood silent for,
I am the mother.
I birthed a girl child
In a ring of fire tied to a wooden stake
I saw her burn and die at my feet while men laughed,
I screamed for,
I am the mother.
My children are born to die, of cold and hunger, disease,
neglect, and war
Endlessly I hold them to my breast and wonder when Peace will
come, for
I am the mother.
I shall be there at every ending be it of woman, or child or man.
I shall weep for each lost life be it humankind or beast for,
I remain the mother.

DOLORES ASHCROFT-NOWICKI

It is true that the church seeks ideals of peace,
but it discerns different kinds of violence.
In my pastoral letter I recall
how on the peak of Tabor
next to Christ transfigured

the five men who appear—
Moses, Elijah, Peter, James, and John—
are men of violent character,
and they committed terribly violent acts.
Moses killed an Egyptian;
Elijah put to the sword
the prophets who did not adore the true God;
Peter drew his sword against Malchus
to defend Christ;
James and John begged Christ to rain fire
on a town that would not give him lodging.
But I say
Christians are peacemakers,
not because they cannot fight,
but because the prefer the force of peace.

OSCAR ROMERO

Condemnation

Listen to this:
Yesterday six Vietcong came through my village.
Because of this my village was bombed—completely destroyed.
Every soul was killed.
When I come back to my village now, the day after,

There is nothing to see but clouds of dust and the river, still flowing.
The pagoda has neither roof nor altar.
Only the foundations of houses are left.
The bamboo thickets are burned away.

Here in the presence of the undisturbed stars,
In the invisible presence of all the people still alive on earth,
Let me raise my voice to denounce this filthy way,
This murder of brothers by brothers!
I have a question: Who pushed us into this killing of one another?

Whoever is listening, be my witness!
I cannot accept this war,
I never could, I never shall.
I have to say this a thousand times before I am killed.

I feel I am like a bird which dies for the sake of its mate,
Dripping blood from its broken beak, and crying out:
Beware! Turn around and face your enemies—
Ambition, violence, hatred, greed.

Men cannot be our enemies—even men called "Vietcong"!
If we kill men, what brothers will we have left?
With whom shall we live then?

THICH NHAT HANH

All Quiet on the Western Front

The silence spreads. I talk and must talk. So I speak to him and say to him: "Comrade, I did not want to kill you. If you jumped in here again, I would not do it, if you would be sensible too. But you were only an idea to me before, an abstraction that lived in my mind and called forth its appropriate response. It was that abstraction I stabbed. But now, for the first time, I see you are a man like me. I thought of your hand-grenades, of your bayonet, of your rifle; now I see your wife and your face and our fellowship. Forgive me, comrade. We always see it too late. Why do they never tell us that you are just poor devils like us, that your mothers are just as anxious as ours, and that we have the same fear of death, and the same dying and the same agony—forgive me, comrade; how could you be my enemy? If we threw away these rifles and this uniform you could be my brother like Kat and Albert. Take twenty years of my life, comrade, and stand up—take more, for I do not know what I can even attempt to do with it now."

ERICH MARIA REMARQUE

Arms

I blasted the place.
I had to.
There were orders, a command,
it was certain I should do it.
It was hard. I am stricken.
The bones of her arm
splinters and I would cross
back through them, always have to
remember it like this,
her body once embraced now
broken over gutted
lots, skulls in piles.
I am pierced by the evil.
That someone would tell you
to do it. That you would.
My face won't peel enough
to see it. What is
the failure in us that makes
evil active, the rigid hide,
some reptilian creature
who has survived in the deep
tunnelled undersea becoming more

translucent against the lack of
light that far down.
That far down what is
breeding. I was told
to take up arms against it.
Whose arms, against whose arms.

THERESA BACON

"I" and "you," "us" and "them," "winning" and "losing," "victor" and "vanquished"—these are no more than the tricks of the mind exiled from the heart. The face we see before us is no other than our own, the person we see before us is ourselves in another guise. What else can we do but open our hearts, what else do we need to do?

CHRISTINA FELDMAN

Think of what a world we could build if the power unleashed in war were applied to constructive tasks! One-tenth of the energy that the various belligerents spent in the war, a fraction of the money they exploded in hand grenades and poison gas, would suffice to raise the standard of living in every country and avert the economic catastrophe of worldwide unemployment. We must be prepared to make the same heroic sacrifices for the cause of war. There is no task that is more important or closer to my heart.

ALBERT EINSTEIN

Prayer is a necessity. Without it we see only our point of view, our own righteousness, and ignore the perspective of our enemies. Prayer breaks down those distinctions. To do violence to others, you must make them enemies. Prayer, on the other hand, makes enemies into friends. When we have brought our enemies into our hearts in prayer, it becomes most difficult to maintain the hostility necessary for violence. In bringing them close to us, prayer serves to protect our enemies. Thus prayer undermines the propaganda and policies of governments designed to make us hate and fear our enemies. By softening our hearts toward our adversaries, prayer can become treasonous. Fervent prayer for our enemies is a great obstacle to war and the feelings that lead to it.

JIM WALLIS

A Prayer of Peace Among the Children of Abraham

You Who live without slumber or sleep,
You Who contain all that is in the heavens and the earth,
You Who know all our actions,
while we grasp but a fraction of Your knowledge,
Guide us to the path of peace through example of Your prophet Abraham.

Just as Abraham marveled at the stars, the moon, and the sun,
only to see beyond and behind them You,
So may we look beyond the divisions that turn religions into false gods, veiling us from their Author, veiling us from You.

Just as Abraham hesitated not to offer his son, Isaac (Ishmael),*
only to have the bare knife stilled by You,
So may we whose armies clashed at night on Abraham's land,
killing countless innocents, victimizing others,
may we now listen for Your voice,
and guided by Your will,
be spared the pain of further bloodletting.

In Judaism is the star of David. Let it be the star of peace shining through the land of Israel and beyond.

*According to some Muslim traditions, it was Ishmael, not Isaac, who was offered as a near sacrifice to the God of Abraham.

In Christianity is the shepherd of peace. Let his reign begin
for all your children called to be his flock;
from every nation peace their motto be.
In Islam is the abode of peace. Let it expand and expand
engulfing all claimants to Abraham's faith—
be they Jews,
be they Christians,
and also, in Your mercy,
be they Muslims.

BRUCE B. LAWRENCE

Reconciliation

Word over all, beautiful as the sky,
Beautiful that war and all its deeds of carnage must
in time be utterly lost,
That the hands of the sisters Death and Night incessantly
softly wash again, and ever again, this soil'd world;
For my enemy is dead, a man divine as myself is dead,
I look where he lies white-faced and still in the
coffin—I draw near,
Bend down and touch lightly with my lips the white face
in the coffin.

WALT WHITMAN

We must be saved by the final form of love which is forgiveness.

REINHOLD NIEBUHR

God created through love and for love. God did not create anything except love itself, and the means to love. He created love in all its forms. He created beings capable of love from all possible distances.

SIMONE WEIL

Those who have brought tears to so many homes,
those who have stained themselves
with the blood of so many murders,
those who have hands soiled with tortures,
those who have calloused their consciences,
who are unmoved
to see under their boots a person abased,
suffering,
perhaps ready to die.
To all of them I say:
No matter your crimes.
They are ugly and horrible,

and you have abased the highest dignity
of a human person,
but God calls you
and forgives you.

Oscar Romero

As God's chosen ones, holy and beloved, clothe yourselves with compassion, kindness, humility, meekness, and patience.

Bear with one another and, if anyone has a complaint against another, forgive each other; just as the Lord has forgiven you, so you also must forgive.

Above all, clothe yourselves with love, which binds everything together in perfect harmony.

Colossians 3:12–14

Forgive do I creatures all, and let all creatures forgive me.
Unto all have I amity, and unto none enmity.

Jainist Prayer

Blessed are you, O God of the Universe,
for you have bound us together in a common life
on this fragile planet.
We confess and offer before you
our misperceptions, our hatred, our bigotry, and our deceit.
Grant us understanding that is grounded in love,
and reconciliation that grows out of humility.
Open our hearts to the possibility and newness
of your Covenant Word.
In the Name of the One God who is
Creator, Redeemer, and Sanctifier,
world without end,
Amen.

MARTIN BELL

But I say to you that listen, Love your enemies, do good to those who hate you, bless those who curse you, pray for those who abuse you.

If anyone strikes you on the cheek, offer the other also; and from anyone who takes away your coat do not withhold even your shirt.

LUKE 6:27

If you cannot do unto others
what you would that they should do to you,
at least do not unto them
what you would not that they should do unto you.
If you would not be made to work ten hours at a stretch in factories or in mines,
if you would not have your children hungry, cold and ignorant,
if you would not be robbed of the land that feeds you,
if you would not be shut up in prisons
and sent to the gallows or hanged for committing an unlawful deed
through passion or ignorance,
if you would not suffer wounds
nor be killed in war—
do not do this unto others.

All this is so simple and straightforward,
and admits of so little doubt,
that it is impossible for the simplest child not to understand,
nor for the cleverest man to refute it.
It is impossible to refute this law,
especially because this law is given to us,
not only by all the wisest men of the world,
not only by the Man who is considered to be God
by the majority of Christians,

but because it is written
in our minds and hearts.

LEO TOLSTOY

A prominent Jewish prayer concludes "May He who made peace in the heavens grant peace to us on earth." What does it mean to create peace in the heavens? Ancient man looked up into the sky and he saw the sun and the rainclouds. And he would say to himself "How can fire and water, sun and rain co-exist in the same sky? Either the water would put out the fire, or the fire would dry up the water." How do they get along? It must be a miracle. The sun says, "If I dry up the rainclouds, as I probably could, the world will not survive without rain." The clouds say, "If we extinguish the sun, the world will perish in darkness." So the fire and the water make peace, realizing that if either one of them achieved a total victory, the world could not endure.

When we pray for God to grant us the sort of peace He ordained in the heavens, this is the miracle we ask for. How can men and women live together happily? They are opposites; their needs are different, their rhythms are different. It takes a miracle for them to bridge those differences and unite the masculine side of God's image with the feminine side.

How can Arabs and Israelis learn to live together? Irish Catholics and Irish Protestants? Black South Africans and white

South Africans? It takes a miracle for them to realize that if they won, if they had it all and the other side had nothing, the world could not survive their victory. Only by making room for everyone in the world, even for our enemies, can the world survive.

May God who showed us the miracle of Shalom, of making room for each other and giving up the illusion of victory in the heavens, grant a similar miracle to all of us who inhabit the earth.

RABBI HAROLD S. KUSHNER

Meta-Rhetoric

Homophobia
racism
self-definition
revolutionary struggle

the subject tonight for
public discussion is
our love

we sit apart
apparently at opposite ends of a line
and I feel the distance
between my eyes

between my legs
a dry
dust topography of our separation

In the meantime people
dispute the probabilities
of union
They reminisce about the chasmic histories
no ideology yet dares to surmount

I disagree with you
You disagree with me
The problem seems to be a matter of scale

Can you give me the statistical dimensions
of your mouth on my mouth
your breasts resting on my own?

I believe the agenda involves
several inches (at least)
of coincidence and endless recovery

My hope is that our lives will declare
this meeting
open

JUNE JORDAN

It is the enemy who can truly teach us to practice the virtues of compassion and tolerance.

THE DALAI LAMA

You must teach your children that the ground beneath their feet is the ashes of our grandfathers. So that they will respect the land, tell your children that the earth is rich with the lives of our kin. Teach your children what we have taught our children, that the earth is our mother. Whatever befalls the earth, befalls the sons of the earth. If men spit upon the ground they spit upon themselves.

This we know. The earth does not belong to man; man belongs to the earth. This we know. All things are connected like the blood which unites one family. All things are connected.

CHIEF SEATTLE

My Friends—There is one great God and power that hath made the world and all things therein, to whom you and I, and all people owe their being and well-being, and to whom you and I must one day give an account for all that we do in the world; this great God hath written his law in our hearts, by which we are taught and commanded to love and help, and do good to one another, and not to do harm and mischief one to another.

Now this great God hath been pleased to make me concerned in your parts of the world, and the king of the country where I live hath given unto me a great province, but I desire to enjoy it with your love and consent, that we may always live together as neighbors and friends; else what would the great God say to us, who hath made us not to devour and destroy one another, but live soberly and kindly together in the world?

Now I would have you well observe, that I am very sensible of the unkindness and injustice that hath been too much exercised toward you by the people of these parts of the world, who sought themselves, and to make great advantages by you, rather than be examples of justice and goodness unto you, which I hear hath been a matter of trouble to you, and caused great grudgings and animosities, sometimes to the shedding of blood, which hath made the great God angry. But I am not such a man, as is well known in my own country; I have great love and regard toward you, and I desire to win and gain your love and friendship, by a kind, just, and peaceable life.

I am your loving friend.

William Penn

The peace of one individual is small. The peace of many people together is big. When we see ourselves as separate from our community and from nature, then violence and strife arise. It is only when we understand our part in an overall unity that there is the possibility of peace on a large scale.

DENG MING DAO

Put things in order, listen to my appeal, agree with one another, live in peace; and the God of love and peace will be with you.

2 CORINTHIANS 13:11

We regard our living together not as an unfortunate mishap
warranting endless competition among us
but as a deliberate act of God
to make us a community of brothers and sisters
jointly involved in the quest for a composite answer
to the varied problems of life.

STEVEN BIKO

This and this alone
Is true religion—
To serve thy brethren:

This is sin above all other sin,
To harm thy brethren:

In such a faith is happiness,
In lack of it is misery and pain:

Blessed is he who swerveth not aside
From this strait path:
Blessed is he whose life is lived
Thus ceaselessly in serving God:

By bearing others' burdens,
And so alone,
Is life, true life, to be attained:

Nothing is hard to him who, casting self aside,
Thinks only this—
How may I serve my fellow-men.

TULSIDAS*

*Translated from the Sanskrit by Mohandas Gandhi

We still don't know how to put morality ahead of politics, science and economics. We are still incapable of understanding that the only genuine backbone of all our actions—if they are to be moral—is responsibility. Responsibility to something higher than my family, my country, my company, my success. Responsibility to the order of Being, where all our actions are indelibly recorded and where, and only where, they will be properly judged.

VÁCLAV HAVEL

All celestial harmony is
a mirror of divinity
and
man
is a mirror of all
the miracles of God.

ST. HILDEGARD OF BINGEN

Peace NaNa

Iba'che NaNa,* Womb of Creation.
She Who Gave Birth to All Things.
From your dark depths the first spark came into Being.
Your luminous Egg exploded in the midst of eternal night,
its joyous dance formed the great lights.

You Who Gave Us Sun and Moon, Earth and Sky, Body and Spirit.
Awaken from your sleep, Deep Night.
Lift your eyelids and see our plight.
The children of Earth are in need of your guidance;
they await the feel of your hand.
They roll their eyes in great suspicion,
in anger and fear they strike out.
Their hearts are hard, their hands are trembling.
Amidst the rubble of war, they cry out.

Hear me Great Mother, hear your daughter.
Open your starlit thighs. Draw us back into your vulva.
Mix us, stir us, roll and squeeze;
mold our heads,
pat our behinds.
Change us, every cell and spirit 'til Peace possesses our minds.

*A Yoruba term of great respect

Blow your perfumed breath upon us,
wash us in the deep blue sea.
Suckle us on milk and honey,
oil us with the balm of love.

Return us then to this green garden,
Oh Beautiful, Generous Mother,
but this time
give us also the wisdom to see your reflection in each other.

LUISAH TEISH

Silence Abides

Everything changes, everything passes,
Things appearing, things disappearing.
But when all is over—everything having appeared and
having disappeared,
Being and extinction both transcended.—
Still the basic emptiness and silence abides,
And that is blissful Peace.

MAHA PRAJNA PARAMITA HRIDAYA

i was cold / i was burning up / a child
& endlessly weaving garments for the moon
with my tears
I found god in myself
& i loved her / i loved her fiercely

NTOZAKE SHANGE

Psalm 131

Lord, my mind is not noisy with desires,
and my heart has satisfied its longing.
I do not care about religion
or anything that is not you.
I have soothed and quieted my soul,
like a child at its mother's breast.
My soul is as peaceful as a child
sleeping in its mother's arms.

TRANSLATED BY STEPHEN MITCHELL

Peace must begin within self before there can come action or self application in a way to bring peace—even in thine own household, in thine own vicinity, in thine own state or nation.

EDGAR CAYCE

Everyman is me, I am his brother. No man is my enemy. I am Everyman and he is in and of me. This is my faith, my strength, my deepest hope and my only belief.

KENNETH PATCHEN

First there must be order and harmony within your own mind. Then this order will spread to your family, then to the community, and finally to your entire kingdom. Only then can you have peace and harmony.

CONFUCIUS

I don't feel I'm in their clutches anyway, whether I stay or am sent away. I find all that talk is so cliché-ridden and naive and I can't go along with it anymore. I don't feel in anybody's clutches, I feel safe in God's arms, and no matter whether I'm sitting at this beloved old desk now or in a bare room in the Jewish district or perhaps in a labor camp under SS guards—I shall always feel safe in God's arms.

ETTY HILLESUM

God guides those who seek His good pleasure into the ways of peace, bringing them out from the shadows into the light by His act of will and guiding them into a straight path.

QUR'AN

Thou movest us to delight in praising Thee, for Thou hast formed us for Thyself, and our hearts are restless till they find rest in Thee.

ST. AUGUSTINE OF HIPPO

Praying Next to a Holocaust Survivor
(Yom Kippur, 5745)

We recited confession
I was astounded
What was he confessing, and why?
Who was asking forgiveness from whom?
We recited the penitential prayers
I saw
the shadow that crossed his face
memories welling up from the depths.
"Therefore, put fear of You into all Your creatures"—
an anger hidden in his body
Why were they not afraid?
Why did He not put fear into them?
We recited the Sh'ma*
I was ashamed

*A daily Hebrew prayer that begins "Hear, O Israel, the Lord our God . . ."

Who am I to recite Sh'ma next to him?
What is my faith next to his?
"Our Father, our King"—
he has the advantage
Job, faithful servant
'How horrible are the terrible deeds You have set aside
for those that fear You
an eye other than Yours has seen, O God.'
"Act for the sake of suckling infants who have not sinned"—
Were they my children?
Woe unto the eyes that saw such things.
I do not want to see; I cannot.
He too does not want to see but he is compelled,
and I am compelled in his compulsion
My son . . . my daughter . . .
"If as children, if as servants"—
Lord, we really and truly only wanted to be
good children, loyal servants
Even now,
"we are Your children and You are our Father"
"we are Your servants and You are our Sovereign"
Have mercy on us; have pity.
Heal us, and we shall be healed.

DAVID R. BLUMENTHAL

God makes his home in you. They are not empty words. It is true. "Make your home in me, as I make mine in you." This is prayer. Isn't this the answer to all our yearning, our searching, our anguish, to all the longing, the incompleteness of our lives and of our loving? Until we dwell in him and allow him to dwell in us we shall be strangers to peace.

MOTHER FRANCES DOMINICA

I give you only one bit of advice: do not think that you will ever attain the prayer of quiet by dint of your own efforts. They would be unavailing, and after having had devotion, you would become cold. But simply and humbly, for humility obtained everything, say: thy will be done.

ST. TERESA OF AVILA

One of the basic points is kindness. With kindness, with love and compassion, with this feeling that is the essence of brotherhood, sisterhood, one will have inner peace. This compassionate feeling is the basis of inner peace.

THE DALAI LAMA

It is clear that peace is as fragile as the human condition of which it is a part. Temptations abound to lessen its realization. Not least of which is the ego that seeks its own power, and the greed hidden in its shadows.

ALBERT HUERTA, S.J.

Seeing the rest of the world filled full of iniquity, the lover of justice will be content to keep his own life on earth untainted by wickedness and impious actions, so that he may leave this world with a fair hope of the next, at peace with himself and God.

PLATO

As I work with millions of people, teaching them the medical effects of nuclear war, I find that their instinct for survival overcomes their primitive nationalistic urges. The survival instinct is the strongest physiological drive we possess, more powerful than those for eating or reproduction. People faced with imminent prospects of extinction suddenly become transformed when they realize that in order to save themselves and those they love, they must help others who are totally alien to them. These feelings are possessed by everyone. We were not put on earth to make ourselves happy. The path to true happiness lies in helping others.

HELEN CALDICOTT

Only when peace lives within each of us, will it live outside of us. We must be the wombs for a new harmony. When it is small, peace is fragile. Like a baby, it needs nurturing attention. We must protect peace from violence and perversion if it is to grow. We must be strong to do this. But force, even in the name of honor, is always tragic. Instead, we must use the strength of wisdom and conscience. Only that power can nurture peace in this difficult time.

DENG MING DAO

God, like a sojourner called forth from your garden, I abide upon this maternal soil to be a transparent messenger of your peace. Therefore, my will and my life I entrust into your hands. Mold me as you see fit for whatever you give me. I am grateful. Whatever you send me, I accept.

Sustain me only with your wisdom and your love so that all whom I meet on this journey home may see through me to you.

CRAIG O'NEILL

You, then, are my workers. You have come from me, the supreme eternal gardener, and I have engrafted you onto the vine by making myself one with you.

Keep in mind that each of you has your own vineyard. But everyone is joined to your neighbors' vineyards without any dividing lines. They are so joined together, in fact, that you cannot do good or evil for yourself without doing the same for your neighbors.

St. Catherine of Siena

The Want of Peace

All goes back to the earth,
and so I do not desire
pride of excess or power,
but the contentments made
by men who have had little:
the fisherman's silence
receiving the river's grace,
the gardener's musing on rows.

I lack the peace of simple things
I am never wholly in place.
I find no peace or grace.

We sell the world to buy fire,
our way lighted by burning men,
and that has bent my mind
and made me think of darkness
and wish for the dumb life of roots.

WENDELL BERRY

Dear God, we give thanks for places of simplicity and peace. Let us find such a place within ourselves. We give thanks for places of refuge and beauty. Let us find such a place within ourselves. We give thanks for places of nature's truth and freedom, of joy, inspiration and renewal, places where all creatures may find acceptance and belonging. Let us search for these places: in the world, in ourselves and in others. Let us restore them. Let us strengthen and protect them and let us create them.

May we mend this outer world according to the truth of our inner life and may our souls be shaped and nourished by nature's eternal wisdom. Amen.

LEUNIG

Last night I stood outside the tent and watched the lake and the sky, and slowly I was overcome by some pathetic yearning and, simultaneously, with a terrible sense of loss and sorrow. It was as if something had died or had been permanently lost—not just to me but to everyone, forever. And I thought of the animals here and the birds and the fish—even of the insects—and of the men and women who were once here, simply, as a natural part of this place—and not just here, but everywhere. And I knew that we had made a separation from them all and from all of this and that we could never, never get it back. All we could do—or hope to do—was to save the little bits of it left. And I thought of all the birds asleep somewhere behind me in their tree—in their forest—and I thought: we were meant to be one thing—not separate, partitioned. We are no better and no worse—no larger and no smaller in worth than any other creature who walks or crawls or flies or swims. We are merely different.

I saw then what I'd come to find and had found: my identity in common with this planet and perhaps, for all I know, with this universe. And I knew then what my prayer is and will remain: make peace with nature, first; make peace with nature . . . now.

Timothy Findley

Stalking Muskrat

Stalking is a pure form of skill, like pitching or playing chess. Rarely is luck involved. I do it right or I do it wrong; the muskrat will tell me, and that right early. Even more than baseball, stalking is a game played in the actual present. At every second, the muskrat comes, or stays, or goes, depending on your skill.

Can I stay still? It is astonishing how many people cannot, or will not, hold still. I could not, or would not, hold still for thirty minutes inside, but at the creek I slow down, center down empty. I am not excited: my breathing is slow and regular. In my brain I am not saying, Muskrat! Muskrat! There! I am saying nothing. If I must hold a position, I do not "freeze." If I freeze, locking my muscles, I will tire and break. Instead of going rigid, I go calm. I center down wherever I am; I find a balance and repose. I retreat—not inside myself, but outside myself, so that I am a tissue of senses. Whatever I see is plenty, abundance. I am the skin of water the wind plays over: I am petal, feather, stone.

I have done this sort of thing so often that I have lost self-consciousness about moving slowly and halting suddenly; it is second nature to me now. And I have often noticed that even a few minutes of this self-forgetfulness is tremendously invigorating. I wonder if we do not waste most of our energy just by spending every waking minute saying hello to ourselves.

Martin Buber quotes an old Hasid master who said, "When you walk across the fields with your mind pure and holy, then from all the stones, and all growing things, and all animals, the sparks of their soul come out and cling to you, and then they are purified and become a holy fire in you."

ANNIE DILLARD

A Prayer for Peace

Eternal wellspring of peace—
May we be drenched with the longing for peace
that we may give ourselves over to peace
until the earth overflows with peace
as living waters overflow the seas.

נִשְׂאַל מֵעֵין הַשָּׁלוֹם:
יִזַּל כַּטַּל
יַעֲרֹף כַּמָּטָר הַשָּׁלוֹם.
וְנַקְדִּישׁ חַיֵּינוּ לְהַגְשָׁמָתוֹ
עַד שֶׁתִּמְלָא הָאָרֶץ בּוֹ
כַּמַּיִם לַיָּם מְכַסִּים.

MARCIA FALK

Father, in the morning of this new day, I seek your shalom. I joyfully and gratefully submit every fiber of my being to you and your will. I surrender every corner of my life, every ounce of personal ambition, striving and longing to you and your kingdom. By your grace, I ask for that purity of heart that wills only one thing—your will and glory.

Lord Jesus in the morning of this new day, I seek your shalom. I ask for the grace to make every decision and perform every single act according to the values of your kingdom, according to the model you lived and taught.

And, blessed Holy Spirit, in the morning of this new day, I seek your shalom. I implore you to shower upon me the fullness of your fruits, gifts and power. Please intercede for me with groans too deep for human utterance so that all this day I may live and act for the honor and glory of the God whom I love and adore, Father, Son, and Holy Spirit. Amen.

RONALD J. SIDER

Pray for introspection to bless the citizens of this world that they might stop to think about the possibilities of this life and see and understand the limitation and problems of others. Pray that visions, personal and social, be broadened, that compassion and practicality are joined. Pray that selfishness and aloofness disappear.

OSCAR HIJUELOS

A Prayer for Inner Tranquility

Oh God, why must I struggle every day and every hour to secure that inner peace and deep tranquility which is the very essence of what You desire for me and for all Your children?

Is it my pride or my passions which make true peace an infrequent visitor in my life? Or, is it Your will to seek the purification of my soul by keeping me in disquiet?

The saints have thundered for centuries—let nothing affright you. But oh God, many things do disturb and frighten me. I beg You for deliverance from the demons. I beseech You to give me that peace which You promised to those who at least tried to love You.

St. Ignatius and all the mystics have insisted that unhappiness is not a message from God, but a sign from the Evil One. So, I ask you, Lord, to dispel the sources of Satan and deliver this pilgrim from turmoil and trouble.

In quietness, tranquility and peace let me just rest in Your peaceful presence until the storms of life subside and the vision of Your beauty is all there is. Amen.

ROBERT F. DRINAN, S.J.

Implosions

The world's
not wanton
only wild and wavering

I wanted to choose words that even you
would have to be changed by

Take the word
of my pulse, loving and ordinary
Send out your signals, hoist
your dark scribbled flags
but take
my hand

All wars are useless to the dead

My hands are knotted in the rope
and I cannot sound the bell

My hands are frozen to the switch
and I cannot throw it

The foot is in the wheel

When it's finished and we're lying
in a stubble of blistered flowers

eyes gaping, mouths staring
dusted with crushed arterial blues

I'll have done nothing
even for you?

ADRIENNE RICH

If a man has beheld evil, he may know that it was shown to him in order that he learn his own guilt and repent; for what is shown to him is also within him.

BA'AL SHEM TOV

Oh Lord, merciful and compassionate Lord, am I the one, the one who's created Auschwitz? It's much worse than that he—the German facing me with the death's skull insignia on his cap, his hands deep in the pockets of his black S.S. coat—could have been in my place. It's that I—and this is the paralyzing horror—I could have been there in his place!

Oh Lord, Lord of Auschwitz heavens, illumine my ignorance of your handiwork, so that I might know who is the being within me now delivered to the crematorium—and why?

And who is the being within him delivering me to the crematorium—and why? For you know that at this moment the two of us, dispatcher and dispatched, are equal sons of man, both created by you, in your image.

KA-TZETNIK 135633

Suprapunna asked the Lord Buddha as follows:

"What shall we get rid of if we want peace and happiness? What shall we do to get rid of sorrow? What is the poison that devours all our good thoughts?"

"Kill hatred and thou shalt have peace and happiness. Kill hatred and thou shalt have no more sorrow. It is hatred that devours all thy goodness."

DHYANA

Seek peace in your own place. You cannot find peace anywhere save in your own self. In the psalm we read: "There is no peace in my bones because of my sin." When a man has made peace within himself, he will be able to make peace in the whole world.

RABBI BUNAM

Mindfulness Must Be Engaged

Mindfulness Must Be Engaged

When I was in Vietnam, so many of our villages were being bombed. Along with my monastic brothers and sisters, I had to decide what to do. Should we continue to practice in our monasteries, or should we leave the meditation halls in order to help the people who were suffering under the bombs? After careful reflection, we decided to do both—to go out and help people and to do so in mindfulness. We called it engaged Buddhism. Mindfulness must be engaged. Once there is seeing, there must be acting. Otherwise, what is the use of seeing? We must be aware of the real problems of the world. Then, with mindfulness, we will know what to do and what not to do to be of help. If we maintain awareness of our breathing and continue to practice smiling, even in difficult situations, many people, animals, and plants will benefit from our way of doing things. Are you massaging our Mother Earth every time your foot touches her? Are you planting seeds of joy and peace? I try to do exactly that with every step, and I know that our Mother Earth is most appreciative. Peace is every step. Shall we continue the journey?

THICH NHAT HANH

Singing with Angels

Peace is an act of the heart. But what is the heart? We have a sense of this something within that calls us to feel, and having felt, to open our selves—if only a little—to another living being: as if that soul were a part of our soul, as if his or her mind were our very own. It is a strange experience first to have this tiny belief in the possibility of love, then to find ourselves acting in another person's interests. Sometimes the act must come first, and then the little particle of love will follow. Sometimes we must simply say, "I will make at least one puny effort today to treat another as if we were one, even though I will expect nothing in return." What are the consequences of a path so contrary to the ways of the world? Possibly there is no external reward at all. However, one gift is assured. Should you choose to so proceed, a day will come when you will find yourself singing with angels here on earth. And that song will be:

> I am one with thee
> O thou infinite One.
> I am where thou art.
> I am what thou art.
> I am because thou art.

HUGH PRATHER

Unjust laws exist: shall we be content to obey them, or shall we endeavor to amend them, and obey them until we have succeeded, or shall we transgress them at once? Men generally, under such a government as this, think that they ought to wait until they have persuaded the majority to alter them. They think that, if they should resist, the remedy would be worse than the evil. But it is the fault of the government itself that the remedy *is* worse than the evil. *It* makes it worse. Why is it not more apt to anticipate and provide for reform? Why does it not cherish its wise minority? Why does it cry and resist before it is hurt? Why does it not encourage its citizens to be on the alert to point out its faults, and *do* better than it would have them? Why does it always crucify Christ, and excommunicate Copernicus and Luther, and pronounce Washington and Franklin rebels?

HENRY DAVID THOREAU

We should never forget that everything Adolf Hitler did in Germany was "legal" and everything the Hungarian freedom fighters did in Hungary was "illegal."

MARTIN LUTHER KING, JR.

A society based on the letter of the law and never reaching any higher fails to take advantage of the full range of human possibilities. The letter of the law is too cold and formal to have a beneficial influence on society. Whenever the tissue of life is woven of legalistic relationships, this creates an atmosphere of spiritual mediocrity that paralyzes man's noblest impulses. And it will be simply impossible to bear up to the trials of this threatening century with nothing but the supports of a legalistic structure.

ALEXANDER SOLZHENITSYN

If you want peace, work for justice.

POPE PAUL VI

Time itself is neutral; it can be used either destructively or constructively. More and more I feel that the people of ill will have used time much more effectively than have the people of good will. We will have to repent in this generation not merely for the hateful words and actions of the bad people, but for the appalling silence of the good people. Human progress never rolls in on wheels of inevitability; it comes through the tireless efforts of men willing to be co-workers with God, and without this hard work, time itself becomes an ally of the forces of stagnation.

MARTIN LUTHER KING, JR.

Let us recognize that as with individuals, so with social structures: they can be outwardly orderly yet inwardly violent. And if violence means violating human integrity, then without hesitation we must call violent any social structure that condemns human beings to hopelessness and helplessness, to less than human existence. Further, it is clear that people concerned with non-violence must show not only compassion for the victims of violence but also a determination to change the structures of society that make them objects of compassion.

WILLIAM SLOANE COFFIN

Awakening

I was gentle and peaceful,
a flower.
But gentleness isn't a wall
that hides misery
and I saw injustice,
and strikes and rebellions
by ordinary people
exploded before my astonished eyes.

And instead of absurd pity
and sympathetic hypocrisy

my indignation burst forth
and I felt myself united with my sisters and brothers,
and every strike hurt me,
and every cry struck me
not only in my head or ears
but in my heart.
My white gentleness fell,
dead at the feet of hunger,
I undressed myself, weeping at its veils
and new clothing clung to my flesh.
My arms now in the springtime of struggle,
My red-hot blood protesting,
my body olive green
an incendiary passion consumes me
. . . and nevertheless
I keep feeling as before,
a lover of peace,
I want to fight for it—desperately
because from the beginning
I have dreamt of peace.

LIL MILAGRO RAMIREZ

Over the past few years I have been gravely disappointed with the white moderate . . . who is more devoted to "order" than to justice; who prefers a negative peace which is the absence of tension to a positive peace which is the presence of justice.

MARTIN LUTHER KING, JR.

Come Lord!
Do not smile and say
you are already with us.
Millions do not know you
and to us who do,
what is the difference?
What is the point
of your presence
if our lives do not alter?
Change our lives, shatter
our complacency.
Make your word
flesh of our flesh,
blood of our blood
and our life's purpose.

Take away the quietness
of a clear conscience.
Press us uncomfortably.
For only thus
that other peace is made,
your peace.

DOM HELDER CAMARA

I think that people want peace so much that one of these days government had better get out of their way and let them have it.

DWIGHT D. EISENHOWER

We must work to accept that if we truly want peace we shall have it. The passionate longings of the people cannot forever be denied.

RITA MAE BROWN

To the ordinary man or woman, it seems a hopeless task to influence the policy of the government. But to express the desire for peace effectively, it is essential to show that, whatever the nominal issue, you will oppose any and every war that the folly of governments may be tempted to provoke. Nothing less drastic can be expected to stand firm against the excitement which the approach of war invariably produces. If the friends of peace are to be politically effective, they must be unwilling to listen to arguments tending to show that this war is unlike all other wars, that all the guilt is on the other side, or that the millennium will come if our side is victorious. These things have always been said at the outbreak of a war, and have always been false.

BERTRAND RUSSELL

Seek peace, and pursue it.

PSALM 34:13

The path of prayer leads to the center of peace.

OSCAR WILDE

Prayer and sacrifice must be used as the most effective spiritual weapons in the war against war, and like all weapons, they must be used with deliberate aim: not just with a vague aspiration for peace and security, but against violence and war. This implies that we are also willing to sacrifice and restrain our own instinct for violence and aggressiveness in our relations with other people. We may never succeed in this campaign, but whether we succeed or not, the duty is evident.

THOMAS MERTON

My experience has been that the poor know violence more intimately than most people because it has been a part of their lives, whether the violence of the gun or the violence of want and need. I don't subscribe to the belief that non-violence is cowardice. When people are involved in something constructive, trying to bring about change, they tend to be less violent than those who are not engaged in rebuilding or in anything creative. Non-violence forces one to be creative; it forces any leader to go to the people and get them involved so that they can come forth with new ideas. I think that once people understand the strength of non-violence—the force it generates, the love it creates, the response that it brings from the total community—they will not be willing to abandon it easily.

CESAR CHAVEZ

Nonviolence is not a garment to be put on and off at will. Its seat is in the heart, and it must be an inseparable part of our very being.

MOHANDAS GANDHI

There never was a time when, in my opinion, some way could not be found to prevent the drawing of the sword.

ULYSSES S. GRANT

The question is not whether we will be extremists, but what kind of extremists we will be. Will we be extremists for hate or for love? Will we be extremists for the preservation of injustice or for the extension of justice?

MARTIN LUTHER KING, JR.

We have never preached violence,
except the violence of love,
which left Christ nailed to a cross,
the violence that we must each do to ourselves
to overcome our selfishness
and such cruel inequalities among us.
The violence we preach is not the violence of the sword,
the violence of hatred.
It is the violence of love,
of brotherhood,
the violence that wills to beat weapons
into sickles for work.

OSCAR ROMERO

No one has a right to sit down and feel hopeless. There's too much work to do.

DOROTHY DAY

Father! Before thy throne come,
Not in the panoply of war,
With pealing trump, and rolling drum,
And cannon booming loud and far;
Striving in blood to wash out blood,
Through wrong to seek redress for wrong:
For while tho'rt holy, just and good,
The battle is not to the strong;
But in the sacred name of peace,
Of justice, virtue, love and truth,
We pray, and never mean to cease,
Till weak old age and fiery youth
In freedom's cause their voices raise,
And burst the bonds of every slave;
Till, north and south, and east and west,
The wrongs we bear shall be redressed.

J. M. WHITFIELD*

For he is our peace; in his flesh he has made both groups into one and has broken down the dividing wall, that is, the hostility between us.

EPHESIANS 2:14

*J. M. Whitfield was an African-American abolitionist during the Civil War.

Whether we are speaking of warring couples or nations, it is an extraordinary challenge to move from blaming people, toward understanding patterns and our own part in them. It is a similarly huge challenge that our wish to understand the other party be as great as our wish to be understood. Because I watch some individuals and families meet this challenge in the most difficult of circumstances—and because I live in a world that is transformed daily by remarkable feminist voices—I continue to maintain hope.

HARRIET GOLDHOR LERNER

Sleeping Beauties

The old map-makers
Had to deal with a half-complete picture of reality:
The question, as always, was how to describe it.

Their known world was the tatterdemailion coat
Of a beggar, riddled with holes and empty pockets,
Pleading to be covered.
For the vast mystery of unexplored shores and seas,
The negative space of atlases designed
To hold up the cosmos,

The yawning gaps of geography
The size of vast continents,
(the scope of the unknown you to me),

The early cartographers
Imagined "sleeping beauties,"
As if unmapped territory
Is not a horror to be silenced,
But dream to awaken,
Not an enemy to be vanquished,
But a discovery to embrace.

Then, why the recurring failure of our imaginations?
Why do we fear what we arouse in each other:
All this unknown territory inside us,
All these unseen worlds between us
To be circumnavigated
With the ardor of explorers?

Why can't the emptiness be a wonder to evoke,
A beauty to awake, a peace to share,
In the bramble-entwined castles
We have each fallen asleep in?

If there are no rules for exploration
Between lovers anymore
It is time we measure for ourselves

The rugged coastline,
The deep harbors,
The mysterious coves

No one else has ever seen.

The monsters others imagined there
Might only be beauties waiting to be loved.

PHIL COUSINEAU

History is not kind to us
we restitch it with living
past memory   forward
into desire
into the panic   articulation
of want   without having
or even the promise of getting.

And I dream of our coming together
encircled   driven
not only by love
but by lust for a working tomorrow
the flights of this journey
mapless   uncertain
and necessary as water.

AUDRE LORDE

What is more fluid, more yielding than water?
Yet back it comes again, wearing down the rigid strength
Which cannot yield to withstand it.
So it is that the strong are overcome by the weak,
The haughty by the humble.
This we know
But never learn.

LAO TSE

Prayer to Pax

(Light a silver candle in a circle of wild
flower petals)
Say:
Silver One!
You who are honored three times a year
with humble marches
Maidens honored walks
When even the powerful
wears none of the insignia of their office
as we pray at your public altars
for continued peace.
We are back again.

Put your mighty silver force
your mighty ray of the soul
(if you please)
against the warlovers selfish blindness.
Let war be passé.
Only you can do this.
Then It is done.

(Light a golden candle in the circle of rose petals)
Say:
Golden One!
Yellow sunflowers, heralds of wealth
Milliards of honeybees laden with golden drops
celebrate your holy presence.
Come back to us!
Teach us the ancient arts
of tolerance and fair trade
Pour your wisdom in the drops of honey
So that even the most mean spirited
Will finally be able to feel you.
Make your women especially strong
(if you please)
so that we can endure the torrents of abuse

still our bitter lot of war at home.
As we shall slay the mind's monsters
that harmed us amongst our own kin.
Bring us back the love we deserve.
This you can do.
Then It is done.

(Light a black candle in a circle of dried bones)
Say:
Black One!
You are the peace of death
precious jewel reward
after a life well spent:
Peace unutterable.
We celebrate you with all the
ancestors who have gone before us.
We remember that our time too is but brief.
You need not our kind
to help you hurry death.
You shall surely come
and call our names one by one.
absorb our fears of each other
make our hate darkness
be absorbed by your holy death.

Let your peace not be
the only one we know.
This you can do.
(If you please)
Then It is done.

Silver One
Golden One
Black One
make it so.

ZSUZSANNA BUDAPEST

Whatever God does, the first outburst is always compassion.

MEISTER ECKHART

To confront evil successfully, we as a nation must also confront our own darkness; we must act not as a messiah, filled with undue majesty and certainty, but rather as a healer, filled with compassion, empathy, and humility.

DAVID SPANGLER

A body with cancer is terminally ill, because the cancer cells have gone crazy. They split and increase in an aberrant, autonomous way, without keeping in mind the interest of the organism of which they are a part. Eventually, through their sheer numbers and the speed of their blind growth, they take over and so weaken the immune system, that the body dies. The way I relate to cancer as a healer is not to fight or "kill" the cancer cells, but rather to focus attention on the healthy cells. If the healthy cells can be awakened and enlivened, so that they begin to vibrate at a higher level, the cancer has been known to miraculously and spontaneously leave the body, for no apparent reason. Surely this global body is suffering from terminal cancer, warmakers acting as the crazy cancer cells, taking up more and more space, and overpowering the organic process of life on earth. But I am a healthy cell in this poor sick body, and I'll wager that you are, too. It seems to me that our responsibility as healthy cells, on a daily basis, is simply to raise our vibration and join together for health. I saw us doing this when thousands of us hit the streets together, chanting and singing for peace. I see it in my healing circles, when we join together to drum and sing, awakening the sleeping cells in the body, and jump starting the weakened immune system.

VICKI NOBLE

Blessed are the poor in spirit, for they know the unutterable
beauty of simple things.
Blessed are those who mourn, for they have dared to risk their
hearts by giving of their love.
Blessed are the meek, for the gentle earth shall embrace them
and hallow them as its own.
Blessed are those who hunger and thirst for righteousness, for
they shall know the taste of noble thoughts and deeds.
Blessed are the merciful, for in return theirs is the gift of giving.
Blessed are the pure in heart, for they shall be at one with
themselves and the universe.
Blessed are the peacemakers, for theirs is a kinship with
everything that is holy.
Blessed are those who are persecuted for righteousness' sake,
for the truth will set them free.

F. Forrester Church

Psalm

Father
You are the trunk
We are the branches
When the Ark opens
We stand beside your silver tree
On this side of the earth
Reading your words
Over and over
Raking the coals.

And when we look up
And glimpse the future
Lashed to the mast of an ark
Rolling over the waters
Of a dark sea
We wrap ourselves
Once more
In your garment of light
Your prayer shawl
Woven from the fabric
Of history.

But father
We are still waiting

For the rain that must come
On its own
And for the tree that will spring up
Out of those waters
And bear fruit.

HOWARD SCHWARTZ

Love is not a vague feeling or an abstract idea. When I love someone, I seek what is best for them. If I begin to take the love of Christ seriously, then I will work toward what is best for my neighbor. I will seek to bind up the wounds and bring about healing, no matter what the cost may be.

BILLY GRAHAM

As long as we are on earth, the love that unites us will bring us suffering by our very contact with one another, because this love is the resetting of a Body of broken bones. Even saints cannot live with saints on this earth without some anguish, without some pain at the differences that come between them. There are two things which men can do about the pain of disunion with other men. They can love or they can hate. Hatred recoils from the sacrifice and the sorrow that are the price of this resetting of bones. It refuses the pain of reunion. But love by the acceptance of the pain of reunion, begins to heal all wounds.

THOMAS MERTON

Our works are nothing but works of peace.

MOTHER TERESA

Just as a mother would protect her only child, even at risk of her own life, even so let one cultivate a boundless heart toward all beings.

SHAKYAMUNI BUDDHA

Aphrodite Columba, Great Goddess, Holy Dove of Peace, hear Your daughters as they call to You again after the turning of centuries; for they are humanity's lifegiving mothers. They know the toil of birthing and nurturing. They know war to be a waste of their precious toil, and a desecration of Your earth. Kindly Mother, give Your daughters power to oppose the forces of war, to prevent aggressive destruction, to establish Your laws of peace and kinship. Help women raise their children with teachings of peace. Help men resist the myths of glory in conflict. Help us all to respect life more than conquest. Let the return of the Divine Mother image usher in a new era, as the women of all nations reach out to one another with understanding, under Your symbol. Let those who do not comprehend motherhood hear and obey those that do. Aphrodite Columba, Sacred Dove, let the spiritual needs of those who yearn for You be served at last. May our prayer rise to You as the white dove rises on her wings.

Blessed Be.

BARBARA G. WALKER

Lord, make me an instrument of Thy peace. Where there is hatred, let me sow love; where there is injury, pardon; where there is doubt, faith; where there is despair, hope; where there is sadness, joy; where there is darkness, light.

O Divine Master, grant that I may not so much seek to be consoled, as to console; not so much to be understood, as to understand; not so much to be loved, as to love. For it is in giving that we receive, it is in pardoning that we are pardoned, it is in dying that we are born again to eternal life.

ST. FRANCIS OF ASSISI

For the Quakers

Theirs is the gentle finger on the pulse
Of war's old woe.
Persistent, with the clear unrancored eyes
Of faith, they go
Where disillusion lost the charted way.
Unerringly
They reach across the desperate long miles,
The sullen sea,
And find the thin small fingers in the cold,
And touch, and hold.

BIANCA BRADBURY

Deadline

The night before war begins, and you are still here.
you can stand in a breathless cold
ocean of candles, a thousand issues of your same face
rubbed white from below by clear waxed light.
A vigil. You are wondering what it is
you can hold a candle to.

You have a daughter. Her cheeks curve
like aspects of the Mohammed's perfect pear.

She is three. Too young for candles but
you are here, this is war.
Flames covet the gold-sparked ends of her hair,
her nylon parka laughing in color,
inflammable. It has taken your whole self
to bring her undamaged to this moment,
and waiting in the desert at this moment
is a bomb that flings gasoline in a liquid sheet,
a laundress's snap overhead, wide as the ancient Tigris,
and ignites as it descends.

The polls have sung their opera of assent: the land
wants war. But here is another America,
candle-throated, sure as tide.
Whoever you are, you are also this granite anger.
In history you will be the vigilant dead
who stood in front of every war with old hearts
in your pockets, stood on the carcass of hope
listening for the thunder of its feathers.

The desert is diamond ice and only stars above us here
and elsewhere, a thousand issues of a clear waxed star,
a holocaust of heaven
and somewhere, a way out.

BARBARA KINGSOLVER

Shelter Beneath the Tree

We wouldn't recognize peace if it came leaping into our midst this moment and shook our hands. We haven't a clue what it feels like, what it takes to have it, how the world would look if we did have it.

SONIA JOHNSON

Gathered at the River

As if the trees were not indifferent . . .

A breeze flutters the candles but the trees give off
a sense of listening, of hush.

The dust of August on their leaves.
But it grows dark. Their dark green
is something known about, not seen.

But summer twilight takes away
only color, not form. The tree-forms,
massive trunks and the great domed heads,
leaning in towards us, are visible,

a half-circle of attention.

They listen because the war
we speak of, the human war within ourselves,
the war against ourselves,

the war against earth
against nature,
is a war against them.

The words are spoken
of those who survived a while,
living shadowgraphs, eyes fixed forever
on witnessed horror,

who survived to give
testimony, that no-one
may plead ignorance.
CONTRA NATURAM. The trees,
the trees are not indifferent.

We intone together, NEVER AGAIN,

we stand in a circle,
singing, speaking, making vows,
remembering the dead
of Hiroshima,
of Nagasaki.

We are holding candles: we kneel to set them
afloat on the dark river
as they do
there in Hiroshima. We are invoking

saints and prophets,
heroes and heroines of justice and peace,
to be with us, to help us
stop the torment of our evil dreams . . .

Windthreatened flames bob on the current . . .

They don't get far from shore. But none capsizes
even in the swell of a boat's wake.

The waxy paper cups sheltering them
catch fire. But still the candles
sail their gold downstream.

And still the trees ponder our strange doings, as if
well aware that if we fail,
we fail also for them:
if our resolves and prayers are weak and fail

there will be nothing left of their slow and innocent
wisdom,
no roots,
no bole nor branch,

no memory
of shade,
of leaf,

no pollen.

DENISE LEVERTOV

In days to come
the mountain of the Lord's house
shall be established as the
highest of the mountains,
and shall be raised above the hills;
all the nations shall stream to it.

He shall judge between the nations,
and shall arbitrate for many peoples;
they shall beat their swords into plowshares,
and their spears into pruning hooks;

nation shall not lift up sword against nation,
neither shall they learn war any more.

Isaiah 2:2,4

A Woman's Prayer for Peace

When I think of peace, I think of a world where human beings are no longer brutalized on account of such accidents of birth as sex, race, religion, or nationality. For me, peace is a way of structuring human relations where daily acts of kindness and caring are tangibly rewarded. It is a way of thinking, feeling, and acting where our essential interconnection with one another is truly honored.

I pray for a world where we live in partnership rather than domination; where "man's conquest of nature" is recognized as suicidal and sacrilegious; where power is no longer equated with the blade, but with the holy chalice: the ancient symbol of the power to give, nurture, enhance life. And I not only pray, but actively work, for the day when it will be so.

Riane Eisler

I suggest our best metaphor for peace is an ancient one—the wrestling match. The Greeks visualized peace as a form of loving combat, a contest, or "agon" between well matched and respectful opponents. They applied the word "agon" equally to a wrestling match and a verbal dialogue. Their highest vision was of a world in which the impulse to war might be gentled in an arena where men and women competed for glory. They thought of conflict as creative and strengthening so long as it was rule governed. When I visualize peace I think of nations wrestling together. Politics as a playing field. I see enemies facing each other not as evil empires but as worthy opponents who struggle honestly to further their legitimate interests and value systems. I see the US and the USSR trying to learn from each others' strengths and weaknesses, Capitalism and Socialism locked, not in a Holy War, but in a dialogue about the priority of the individual or the community. And let there be rules, world law, and world courts, honored by all, and referees powerful enough to enforce the will of the commonwealth of nations.

SAM KEEN

Let us be united;
Let us speak in harmony;
Let our minds apprehend alike.
Common be our prayer;
Common be the end of our assembly;
Common be our resolution;
Common be our deliberations.
Alike be our feelings;
Unified be our hearts;
Common be our intentions;
Perfect be our unity.

RIG VEDA

Prayer to Ceres and Pax

Long time did wars engage mankind; the sword was handier than the plowshare; the plough ox was ousted by the charger; hoes were idle, rakes were turned into javelins, and a helmet was made from a heavy tool. Thanks be to the gods and to thy house! Under your foot long time War has been laid in chains. Yoke the ox, commit the seed to the ploughed earth. Peace is the nurse of Ceres, and Ceres is the foster-child of Peace.

OVID

Memories of War, Memories of Peace

We prayed for peace all right.
Every day. May '40 till May '45.
A little ways into Mass, the same old Latin prayer,
dull as the drone of the bombers overhead every night,
drilled into the memory for good:

Deus, auctor pacis et amator,
quem nosse vivere, cui servire regnare est;
protege ab omnibus impugnationibus supplices tuos:
ut qui in defensione tua confidimus,
nullius hostilitatis arma timeamus.

God, you Maker of Peace and its Lover,
to know you is to live, to serve you is to be in power.
We depend on your mercy; defend us from every kind of assault.
For if we trust in your protection,
no enemy violence will intimidate us.

(Never mind the rosaries muttered at home every night.)

Prayers for peace all right,
but as we learned from what we suffered,
they turned into prayers for liberation from the real enemies:
fear, and the self-absorption it breeds.

Early December '44,
just over two months into the final famine.
My father, thin as a rake, returns after dark,
after curfew—the nerve.
He and a friend had left to find food, a week before,
out in the country, fifty miles away,
riding bikes with no tires on them,
not even the Germans would want to steal them.

I can still see what he brought,
wrapped in newsprint and burlap:
six pounds of beef bone in,
six pounds of dried peas,
ten pounds of potatoes,
too much to believe.

Before we knew what was up, mother had put three
pounds of meat,
one whole pound of peas, and two or three
pounds of potatoes aside.

"These go to the neighbors," she said.
"Once you keep everything for yourself you are dead."

To know you is to live.
To serve you is to be in power.

Peace the world cannot give.
Peace more powerful than all our violence.

FRANS JOZEF VAN BEECK, S.J.

From that which we fear, make us fearless.
O bounteous One, assist us with your aid.

May the atmosphere we breathe
breathe fearlessness into us:
fearlessness on earth
and fearlessness in heaven!
May fearlessness surround us
above and below!

May we be without fear
by night and by day!
Let all the world be my friend!

ATHARVA VEDA XIX

All that is in the heavens and on the earth gives praise to God. His is the kingdom and His the praise and His the will that has power over all things. He it is who created you. There are both unbelievers and believers among you and God is watchful over all your actions. With truth He created the heavens and the earth. He fashioned you and well He made your frame. To Him is your destiny. His knowledge encompasses everything in the heavens and the earth. He knows your hidden secrets and your manifest deeds. God knows the very heart within. QUR'AN

I feel very strongly about peace and always have. I don't like to quarrel myself and admit to real cowardice about even family arguments. Fortunately, I was born into a family which considered quarrelling in poor taste and something never to be indulged in in public. Family arguments were permitted after meals as we all grew older. Mother withdrew regularly from them as we pushed back our chairs after dinner and finished the coffee and the wine and sometimes brandy. Mother always listened in the next room. The door was carefully left open, and we spoke clearly and well so that she could hear, but she never added any comments.

This was the result of years of training, which began by the time I was four. When my mother insisted that she would never quarrel as did all the Kennedys, Father insisted in turn that they never quarrelled but that they did love to argue. Therefore and from that early age on until now, I always know instinctively the difference between an argument and a quarrel, and while I enjoy the first to the hilt, I can truly say that I avoid the last like the plague it is.

While we all were in school from the first grade to college and then beyond, we never mentioned sex, money, or politics until dessert and coffee were finished and Mother had withdrawn. Then the affairs of the world were settled and the talk was often good as well as lengthy. I can well remember the first long talks we had about the schools and teachers and suchlike after lunch when Father had a half hour free before he went down to put the paper to bed by three o'clock, and my little sister Anne and I did not have to go back to school until two o'clock. Then later, marriages and children and divorces and even wars were discussed, but always peacefully. That is, without raised voices or violent gestures. Very rarely, towards the end of a family argument, my brother David would storm from the room and slam the door. Father would sigh heavily, then sometimes we would change the subject. David would return before we broke up the discussion or argument so that we could all say good night together to Mother, who would pretend not to have heard the slammed door and never questioned its cause.

By now in my life, I have no real need to avoid such arguments. There is no chance of even a mild quarrel. If there were I would flee it like the Black Pox, for I feel sure that it would leave me shaking and pale and worn to the bone with anguish. The people I hate are unknown to me, often deliberately, and I thank God for that. Probably a psychiatrist would say that this repressed hatred of certain people in history is a danger to me, but I'm not afraid of it. I shall continue until the day I die to practice peace, although I don't really know what that means, except that it is an avoidance of war and therefore is an admission that war does exist. Whether or not this seems like a living lie it is the only way for me to live—in peace.

M. F. K. FISHER

I want to give and take from my children and husband, to share with friends and community, to carry out my obligations to man and to the world, as a woman, as an artist, as a citizen. But I want first of all—in fact, as an end to these other desires—to be at peace with myself. I want a singleness of eye, a purity of intention, a central core to my life that will enable me to carry out these obligations and activities as well as I can.

ANNE MORROW LINDBERGH

O Lord, support us all the day long, until the shadows lengthen and the evening comes, and the world is hushed, and the fever of life is over, and our work is done. Then in thy mercy grant us a safe lodging, and a holy rest, and peace at the last.

JOHN HENRY NEWMAN

The Lake Isle of Innisfree

I will arise and go now, and go to Innisfree,
And a small cabin build there, of clay and wattles made:
Nine bean-rows will I have there, a hive for the honey-bee,
And live alone in the bee-loud glade.

And I shall have some peace there, for peace comes dropping
slow,
Dropping from the veils of the morning to where the cricket
sings;
There midnight's all a glimmer, and noon a purple glow,
And evening full of the linnet's wings.

I will arise and go now, for always night and day
I hear lake water lapping with low sounds by the shore;
While I stand on the roadway, or on the pavements grey,
I hear it in the deep heart's core.

W. B. YEATS

Prayer to Venus

Cause the savage works of war to sleep and be still
over every sea and land.

For thou alone canst delight mortals with quiet peace,
since Mars mighty in battle rules
the savage works of war,
who often casts himself upon thy lap
wholly vanquished by the everliving wound of love,
and thus looking upward with shapely neck thrown back
feeds his eager eyes with love,

Gaping upon thee, goddess, and as he lies back
his breath hangs upon thy lips.
There as he reclines, goddess,
upon thy sacred body,
do thou, pending around him from above,
pour from thy lips sweet coaxings,
and for thy Romans, illustrious one,
crave quiet peace.

LUCRETIUS

There never was a good war or a bad peace.

BENJAMIN FRANKLIN

The goal of great politics, of true politics, is this: the recognition of all the nationalities, the restoration of the historical unity of nations and the uniting of the latter to civilization by peace.

VICTOR HUGO

The people of the earth having agreed
that the advancement of man
in spiritual excellence and physical welfare
is the common goal of mankind;
that universal peace is the prerequisite
for the pursuit of that goal;
that justice in turn is the prerequisite of peace,
and peace and justice stand or fall together;
that iniquity and war inseparably spring
from the competitive anarchy of the national states;
that therefore the age of nations must end,
and the era of humanity begin.

WORLD CONSTITUTION*

*Preamble to the preliminary draft (1948)

He goes to the edge of the cliff and turns his face to the rising sun, and scatters the sacred corn-meal. Then he prays for all the people. He asks that we may have rain and corn and melons, and that our fields may bring us plenty. But these are not the only things he prays for. He prays that all the people may have health and long life and be happy and good in their hearts. And Hopis are not the only people he prays for. He prays for everybody in the whole world—everybody. And not people alone; Lololomai prays for all the plants. He prays for everything that has life. That is how Lololomai prays.

LOLOLOMAI

People are bound, not by walls and frontiers; a country is made secure, not by mountains and rivers; an empire is strong, not by force of arms. Those who find the right way have many to help them; those who lose the right way have few to help them. When there are few to help, even families revolt against each other. When there are many to help, the whole empire is as one.

MENG TZU (MENCIUS)

A king is not saved by his great army;
a warrior is not delivered by his great strength.
The war horse is a vain hope for victory,
and by its great might it cannot save.

Psalm 33:16–17

This world abounds in war horses; let the day come when they will be used only to fertilize fields. Our nations hold a multitude of weapons; let us pray that they be shunned as omens of evil. People yearn for power; let us hope that more and more of us will find contentment in our daily lives.

Let us listen to our own prayers. It is we who will make them real.

Deng Ming Dao

There are only two powers in the world—the power of the sword and the power of the spirit. In the long run, the sword will always be conquered by the spirit.

Napoleon Bonaparte

It is the servants of the all-merciful Lord who go about the earth in modesty and who answer: "Peace" when accosted by those who talk to them rudely.

QUR'AN

All that pretend to fight for Christ are deceived; for his kingdom is not of this world, therefore his servants do not fight.

GEORGE FOX

I am a soldier of Christ; I cannot fight.

ST. MARTIN OF TOURS

The Brahmin

Him I call indeed a Brahmin who without hurting any creatures, whether feeble or strong, does not kill nor cause slaughter. Him I call indeed a Brahmin who is tolerant with the intolerant, mild with the violent, and free from greed among the greedy. Him I call indeed a Brahmin from whom anger and hatred, pride

and hypocrisy have dropped like a mustard seed from the point
of a needle.
Him I call indeed a Brahmin who utters true speech, instructive and free from harshness, so that he offend no one.
Him I call indeed a Brahmin who takes nothing in the world that is not given him, be it long or short, small or large, good or bad.

DHAMMAPADA

This is the field where the battle did not happen,
where the unknown soldier did not die.
This is the field where grass joined hands,
where no monument stands,
and the only heroic thing is the sky.

Birds fly here without any sound,
unfolding their wings across the open.
No people killed—or were killed—on this ground
hallowed by neglect and an air so tame
that people celebrate it by forgetting its name.

WILLIAM STAFFORD

I am Dekanawida and with the Five Nations' confederate lords I plant the Tree of the Great Peace. . . . Roots have spread out from the Tree of the Great Peace . . . and the name of these roots is the Great White Roots of Peace. If any man or any nation outside of the Five Nations shall show a desire to obey the laws of the Great Peace . . . they may trace the roots to their source . . . and they shall be welcomed to take shelter beneath the Tree . . .

IROQUOIS CONSTITUTION

Oh Great Mystery,
We give thanks, for the natural world we see.
All the Creatures, Stones, and Plants
Who show us how to be.
We learn their lessons, seek their truths,
Return our loving praise,
We honor the peace they show us,
Which guides our human ways.
We ask that we may become like them,
Living in harmony,
And deep within our heart of hearts,
Know the Sacred Mystery.
The Eternal Flame of Love burns bright,
When we look upon Your face,

And see the beauty reflected there,
In every creed and race.
The Sacred Pipe releases these words
To the Sky Nation, there above,
That we may walk in beauty,
As examples of peace and love.

JAMIE SAMS

May we obtain the great Confidence of the View
Where both samsara* and nirvana are one.

May we greatly perfect and strengthen Meditation
Which is naturally resting in the altered state.

May we greatly accomplish the Action
Of Non-Action, which is naturally arrived at.

May we self-find the Dharmakaya**
Which is free of obtaining and abandoning.

KYABJE DUJOM RINPOCHE

*Misery

**Peace on earth

If we are peacemakers, You promise, we will be crowned with the grace of adoption as Your children. This work of peacemaking, for which so great a reward is promised, is itself also a gift from You. For if we have every earthly good and peace is absent, what good are all these fine things when war cuts short their enjoyment? By this, therefore, we can see how greatly You love us, that You bestow the precious reward not on pains and sweat, but on the enjoyment of happiness. Peace is indeed the greatest of the things that bring joy; and this You wish all of us to have in such measure as to keep it not only for ourselves, but to be able to dispense from the overflow of our abundance also to others. For you have said, "Blessed are the peacemakers, for they shall be called children of God."

ADAPTED FROM ST. GREGORY OF NYSSA

Don't Destroy the World

I want the future to extend before me like the horizon
widening as I walk. I want the blue sierra that I planted
squatting over the child in my womb
to grow into a thick tangled hedge
rich with blossoms and bees buzzing like crazy.

I want the smell to make someone's great great
grandchildren
dizzy.

Imagine that we are all born
with the gift of time.

ELLEN BASS

The Peace Prayer

Lead me from death to life, from falsehood to truth.
Lead me from despair to hope, from fear to trust.
Lead me from hate to love, from war to peace.
Let peace fill our heart, our world, our universe.
Peace. Peace. Peace.

ADAPTED FROM THE UPANISHADS BY SATISH KUMAR

Oh Lord, once I was smart enough to know a just war when I saw it, the kind of war you would approve of. I am not so smart anymore. Every war looks evil to me now. And even the war well begun becomes evil before it's over. So let us have no more of just wars; they are the worst kind. Now, at last, give us a just peace. It's time, Lord.

Past time. Time for Shalom. Shalom for our breaking hearts. It's time.

LEWIS SMEDES

Pray ye who suffer tyranny,
When kings are weak to give redress,
To shield you with true mastery,
And succor you in wretchedness,
O merchants, pray in faithfulness,
And hawkers, too, when none may speed
With spices, cloth, wine, salt, and seed
To market-fairs, safe from annoy,
From peril, trouble, and misdeed:
O pray for peace—the soul of joy.

Pray God alone, and he will heed
Our prayer, He will behold our need
Whom war and woes untold destroy:
O come in holiness to plead
And pray for peace—the soul of joy.

CHARLES D'ORLEANS

The Hundred Names

From break of day
Till sunset glow
I toil.
I dig my well,
I plow my field,
And earn my food
And drink.
What care I
Who rules the land
If I
Am left in peace?

ANONYMOUS CHINESE POET*

*Written circa 2300 B.C.E.

Peace is not the product of terror or fear.
Peace is not the silence of cemeteries.
Peace is not the silent result of violent repression.
Peace is the generous, tranquil contribution of all
to the good of all.
Peace is dynamism. Peace is generosity.
It is right and it is duty.

OSCAR ROMERO

The powerful have always been willing to baptize the status quo and name it "peace," and the impotent are regularly accused of being troublemakers when all they seek is justice.

SAM KEEN

Football is war's most apt metaphor. Football thinking prevails where diplomacy is abandoned: team 1 vs. team 2, defense vs. offense, winner vs. loser. Air strikes are likened to touchdowns. Borders are gridiron substitutes. Bunkers hold huddles underground. Generals are coaches and soldiers are players. We who watch on television are the cheerleaders. Pass the popcorn.

Rejecting war means rejecting the idea that someone has to win and someone has to lose. It means understanding that football is a game, that it is no substitute for careful thinking and common sense with risky business at hand. Football is not war and war is not football.

Peace means imagining a way to work out differences through dialogue and negotiation. It means valuing other children as much as our own, citing casualties in one figure without distinguishing between nationalities. Peace is envisioning a solution to the unsolvable. It means thinking the unthinkable, that we might just call a halt, yesterday to war.

MARY E. HUNT

Heavenly Father, heavenly Mother,
Holy and blessed is your true name.
We pray for your reign of peace to come,
We pray that your good will be done,
Let heaven and earth become one.
Give us this day the bread we need,
Give it to those who have none.
Let forgiveness flow like a river between us,
From each one to each one to each one.
Lead us to holy innocence
Beyond the evil of our days—
Come swiftly Mother, Father, come.
For yours is the power and the glory and the mercy:
Forever your name is All in One.

PARKER J. PALMER

Index of First Lines

Acknowledgments

Grateful acknowledgment is made to the following, in order of appearance, for permission to reprint material from the books listed below:

By W. H. Auden, from *The English Auden,* copyright © 1977 by Edward Mendelson, William Meredith, and Monroe K. Spears, Executors of the Estate of W. H. Auden.

By Maria Isabel De Los Angeles Ruano, from *Volcan, Poems from Central America,* copyright © City Lights Books, 1983.

By Nakamura Chio, from *Women Poets of Japan,* copyright © 1977 by Kenneth Rexroth and Ikuko Atsumi. New Direction Books.

By Judith Wright, from *Anthology of Australian Religious Poetry,* copyright © 1986 by Les A. Murray. Collins Dove, a Division of HarperCollins Publishers.

By Mary Fullerton, from *Anthology of Australian Religious Poetry,* copyright © 1986 by Les A. Murray. Collins Dove, a Division of HarperCollins Publishers.

By Mark Twain, from *The War Prayer,* copyright © 1984, Harper & Row, Publishers, Inc.

By Langston Hughes, from *The Panther and the Lash,* copyright © 1967 by Arna Bontemps and George Houston Bass. Published by Alfred A. Knopf, Inc.

By Wilfred Owen, from *The Complete Poems and Fragments of Wilfred Owen,* copyright © 1963 and 1983 by the Executors of Harold Owen's Estate. Published by W. W. Norton & Company, Inc.

By Barbara Ehrenreich, from *The Worst Years of Our Lives,* copyright © 1991, HarperCollins Publishers.

By the Dalai Lama, from *Ocean of Wisdom,* copyright © 1989 by His Holiness the Dalai Lama, Tenzin Gyatso. Published by Harper & Row, Publishers, Inc.

By Daniel Berrigan, S.J., copyright © 1973 by the author.

By Martin Luther King, Jr., from *A Testament of Hope,* copyright © 1986 Coretta Scott King, Executrix of the Estate of Martin Luther King, Jr. Published by HarperCollins Publishers.

By the Dalai Lama, from *Ocean of Wisdom,* copyright © 1989 by His Holiness the Dalai Lama, Tenzin Gyatso. Published by Harper & Row, Publishers, Inc.

By Erich Maria Remarque, from *All Quiet on the Western Front,* copyright © 1967 by Random House.

By Langston Hughes, from *The Panther and the Lash,* copyright © 1967 by Arna Bontemps and George Houston Bass. Published by Alfred A. Knopf, Inc.

By Oscar Romero, from *The Violence of Love,* copyright © 1983 by Harper & Row, Publishers, Inc.

By Thich Nhat Hanh, from *The Collected Poems of Thich Nhat Hanh,* copyright © 1992 by Parallax Press.

By Teresa Bacon, from *Peace or Perish,* copyright © 1983 by Poets for Peace.

"Reply to Critics" by Leo Tolstoy, from *On Civil Disobedience and Non-Violence,* copyright © 1967 by Bergman Publishers.

"Meta-Rhetoric" by June Jordan, from *Things that I Do in the Dark,* copyright © 1977 by Random House.

By William Penn, from *Nonviolence in America,* edited by Staughton Lynd, copyright © 1966 by Staughton Lynd. Published by Bobbs Merrill, a Division of Macmillan Publishing Company, Inc.

From *A Buddhist Bible,* copyright © 1938, 1966 by E. P. Dutton and Company, Inc.

By Jonathan Cape Ltd. for *An Interrupted Life, The Diaries of Etty Hillesum, 1941–1943,* copyright © 1983 by Pantheon Books.

By the Dalai Lama, from *Ocean of Wisdom,* copyright © 1989 by His Holiness the Dalai Lama, Tenzin Gyatso. Published by Harper & Row, Publishers, Inc.

By Wendell Berry, from *Collected Poems, 1957–1982,* copyright © 1985, North Point Press.

By Annie Dillard, from *Pilgrim at Tinker Creek,* copyright © 1984, Harper & Row, Publishers, Inc.

By Adrienne Rich, from *The Fact of a Doorframe,* copyright © W. W. Norton & Company, 1984.

By Ka-tzenik 135633, from *Shivitti,* English translation, copyright © 1989 by Eliyah Nike DeNur. Published by Harper & Row Publishers, Inc.

From *A Buddhist Bible,* copyright © 1938, 1966 by E. P. Dutton and Company, Inc.

By Thich Nhat Hanh, from *Peace is Every Step,* copyright © 1991 by Thich Nhat Hanh. Published by Bantam Books.

By Alexander Solzhenitsyn, from *A World Split Apart,* copyright © 1978 by the Russian Social Fund for Persecuted Persons and Their Families. Published by Harper & Row, Publishers, Inc.